Religion For The 21st Century
The Age of New Deism

By Vernon L. Gowdy III

Published by Newdeism Books, Inc.
2107 County Road 1242
Tuttle, OK 73089

Copyright © 2008 Vernon L. Gowdy III

All Rights Reserved

Printed in the United States of America

ISBN: 978-0-557-31319-8

All rights reserved under the International and Pan-American Copyright Conventions. Without limiting the rights under copyright reserved above, no part of this publication may be reproduced, stored or introduced into a retrieval system, or transmitted, in any form, or by any means (electronic, mechanical, photocopying, recording, or otherwise), without the express written permission of the publisher.

The Digital Millennium Copyright Act makes it illegal to circumvent technologies protecting creative works over the Internet and other digital media.

Cover and Back photograph is a panoramic view of the Orion Nebula taken by NASA's Spitzer and Hubble Space Telescopes.

ACKNOWLEDGEMENTS and FOREWORD

I would like to thank Tom W. Boyd, professor of Philosophy at the University of Oklahoma. After taking his Philosophy of Religion class while pursuing my undergraduate degree in Microbiology, I felt that this class opened my mind about religion and allowed me to find my own path to happiness concerning belief in a Supreme Being. This book gives a brief overview of the major religions throughout the world, discusses the natural religion of Deism and how the advancement of science and technology and possible intelligent life on other planets will change our perception of religion in the 21st century.

INTRODUCTION

Science and Technology has advanced rapidly over the past 100 years and with the 21st century underway it was time to examine the major Religions of the World and explore their similarities and differences. The twelve classical world religions described most often, studied in World Religion classes and used in this book are Christianity, Hinduism, Buddhism, Islam, Judaism, Baha'i Faith, Jainism, Shinto, Confucianism, Sikhism, Taoism and Zoroastrianism.

This book will try to show that Deism, the belief in God or a Supreme Being but denying revealed religion (using a book as a source of one's belief) will play a major role in the revolution of religion for the 21st century. Part Two discusses the history, beliefs and practices of Deism; and covers several of our Deist Founding Fathers such as Benjamin Franklin, Thomas Jefferson, George Washington, Thomas Paine, James Madison, other Famous Deists and a short mention about Freemasons.

Part Three will consider the possibility of intelligent life on other planets and the possibility that the planet's alien intelligence believe in a God or a Supreme Being but have no revealed religion like the Bible or Qur'an and no prophets like Jesus Christ or Mohammed. Discovery of intelligent life on other planets will cause a revolution in religion, causing changes in beliefs of our major religions. Religion on Earth can no longer be the center of the universe's religious beliefs. In addition, the premise that alien intelligence may exist doesn't take away one's belief in a Supreme Being and religion, but rather can change one's interpretation.

Part Four will attempt to show common factors of religion, evolution of religion, science and religion and the future of religion.

Part Five will cover the concept of "New Deism" and its definition, beliefs and practices. New Deism will play a major role in the evolution of religion for the 21st century.

MAJOR RELIGIONS THROUGHOUT THE WORLD

HINDUISM

Hinduism differs from Christianity and other Western religions in that it does not have a single founder, a specific theological system, a single system of morality, or a central religious organization. Hinduism consists of thousands of different religious groups that evolved in India since 1500 BCE.

Hinduism has grown to become the world's third largest religion, after Christianity and Islam, with about 762 million followers. It is the dominant religion in India, Nepal, and parts of Sri Lanka.

EARLY HISTORY OF HINDUISM

Hinduism is derived from the Persian word for Indian. Its roots are traceable to the Indus Valley civilization around 4000 to 2200 CE. Its development was influenced by many invasions over thousands of years. One of the major influences occurred when Indo-Europeans invaded Northern India (around 1500 to 500 BCE) from the steppes of Russian and Central Asia. They brought with them their religion of Vedism. These beliefs became mixed with the indigenous Indian native beliefs.

During the first few centuries CE, many sects were created, each dedicated to a specific deity. Typical among these were the Goddesses Shakti and Lakshmi, and the Gods Skanda and Surya.

SACRED TEXTS

Among the most important of all Hindu sacred texts are the Vedas: the Rig Veda, Sama Veda, Yajur Veda and Atharva Veda. The Vedas are the oldest texts of Hindu literature, stemming from an oral tradition believed to go back to at least 1500 BCE. First written down in Vedic, an early form of Sanskrit, around 600 BCE, the forms we have originate from texts written around 300 BCE. The Vedas are the ultimate scriptural authority for Hindus. It's words and wisdom permeates Hindu thought ritual and meditation. The Rig Veda is the oldest and most important of the Vedas with a collection of over a thousand hymns.

Another group of primary texts is the Upanishadas. They were written between 800 and 400 BCE and keep the Vedic philosophy in their writings and they discuss how the soul (Atman) can be united with the ultimate truth (Brahman) through contemplation, mediation and the doctrine of Karma (cumulative effects of a persons' actions).

The Mahabharata, were written 540 to 300 BCE, and have been attributed to the sage Vyasa. They record "the legends of the Bharatas, one of the Aryan tribal groups." The Bhagavad Gita is the sixth book of the Mahabharata. The Bhagavad Gita is the culmination of Hindu thought in a short series of chapters relating between a conversation between a warrior Arjun and the God Krishna.

Another important text is the Ramayana, dated to the first century CE and has been attributed to the poet Valmiki.

Other texts include the Brahmanas, the Sutras and the Aranyakas.

HINDU BELIEFS AND PRACTICES

At the heart of Hinduism is the monotheistic principle of Brahman, that all reality is a unity and the entire universe is one divine entity. Deity is simultaneously visualized as a triad: 1) Brahma the Creator who is continuing to create new realities. 2) Vishnu, the Preserver, who preserves these new creations. Whenever dharma (eternal order, righteousness, religion, law and duty) is threatened Vishnu travels from heaven to earth in one of ten incarnations and 3.) Shiva, the Destroyer, is at times compassionate, erotic and destructive.

Simultaneously, many hundreds of Hindu Gods and Goddesses are worshipped as various aspects of that unity. Depending upon ones view, Hinduism can be looked upon as a monotheistic, trinitarian or polytheistic religion.

Hinduism has four main denominations — Vaishnavism, Saivism, Saktism and Smartism. These sects are represented by a high god, Shaivism by Shiva, Vaishnavism by Vishnu and Shaktism by Shakti. Various sects of Hinduism have evolved into separate religious movements, including Hare Krishna and Sikhism.

The following nine beliefs, offer a simple summary of Hindu spirituality. 1) Belief in the divinity of the Vedas, the world's most ancient scripture, and venerate the Agamas as equally revealed. These primordial hymns are God's word and the bedrock of Sanatana Dharma, the eternal religion that has neither beginning nor end. 2) Belief in one, all-pervasive Supreme Being that is both immanent and transcendent, both Creator and Unmanifest Reality. 3) That the universe undergoes endless cycles of creation, preservation and dissolution. 4) Belief that the soul reincarnates, evolving through many births until all karmas have resolved, and moksha, spiritual knowledge and liberation from the cycle of rebirth, is attained. Not a single soul will be eternally deprived of this destiny. 5) Belief in karma, the law of cause and effect by which each individual creates his own destiny by his thoughts, words and deeds. 6) Belief that divine beings exist in unseen worlds and that temple worship, rituals, sacraments as well as personal devotionals create a communion with these devas and Gods. 7) Belief that a spiritually awakened master, or satguru, is essential to know the Transcendent Absolute, as are personal discipline, good conduct, purification, pilgrimage, self-inquiry and mediation. 8) Belief that all life is sacred, to be loved and revered, and therefore practice ahimsa, "noninjury." 9) Belief that no particular religion teaches the only way to salvation above all others, but that all genuine religious paths are facets of God's Pure Love and Light, deserving tolerance and understanding.

THE CASTE SYSTEM

The Rig Veda defined five social castes. Ones caste

determined the range of jobs or professions from which one could choose. Marriages normally took place within the same caste. One normally was of the same caste as one's parents. In decreasing status, the five castes are Brahmins (the priests and academics), Kshatriyas (military), Vaishyas (farmers and merchants), Sudras (peasants and servants) and Harijan (the outcasts, commonly known as the untouchables).

Although law abolished the caste system in 1949, it remains a significant force throughout India, particularly in the south. Humans are perceived as being trapped in samsara, a meaningless cycle of birth, life, death and rebirth. Karma is the accumulated sum of ones good and bad deeds. Karma determines how you will live your next life. Through pure acts, thoughts and devotion, one can be reborn at a higher level. Eventually, one can escape samsara and achieve enlightenment. Bad deeds can cause a person to be reborn at a lower level, or even as an animal. The unequal distribution of wealth, prestige and suffering are seen as natural consequences for ones previous acts, both in this life and in previous lives.

BUDDHISM

Buddhism is the fourth largest religion in the world, being exceeded in numbers only by Christianity, Islam and Hinduism. Buddhism revolves around the central figure of the Buddha (meaning, "awakened one"). This usually refers to the First Buddha, who is said to have lived around 563 BCE to 483 BCE Prince Siddhartha Guatama, the First Buddha, was born around 563 BCE in Lumbini, which is in modern-day Nepal to Suddhodana of the Guatama Clan, who himself was king of the Shakya tribe. At the age of 29, he left his wife, children and political involvements in order to seek truth; this was an accepted practice at the time for some men to leave their family and lead the life of an ascetic (hermit; spiritual discipline). He studied Brahmanism, but ultimately rejected it. In 535 BCE, he reached enlightenment and assumed the title Buddha. He is also referred to as the Sakyamuni, (sage of the Sakya clan). He promoted The Middle Way, rejecting both extremes of the mortification of the flesh and of hedonism as paths toward the state of Nirvana (complete bliss, liberation). He had many disciples and accumulated a large public following by the time of his death in his early 80's in 483 BCE.

Two and a half centuries later, a council of Buddhist monks collected his teachings and the oral traditions of the faith into written form, called Tripitaka. This included a very large collection of commentaries and traditions; most are called Sutras (discourses).

BUDDHIST BELIEFS

Buddhism, like most of the great religions of the world, is divided into a number of different traditions.

Buddhism is a religion, which shares few concepts with Christianity. For example, they do not believe in a personal savior, the power of prayer, eternal life in a heaven or hell after death. They do believe in reincarnation: the concept that one must go through many cycles of birth, living and death. After many such cycles, if a person releases their attachment to desire and self, they can attain Nirvana.

Buddhism believes in Four Noble Truths which may be described simply as: a) To be fully understood — the universality of suffering; b) To be abandoned — the desire to have and control things which cause suffering; c) To be made visible — the supreme truth and final liberation of nirvana which is achieved as the cause of suffering is eliminated. The mind experiences complete freedom and liberation; d) to be brought into being — the truth of the eightfold ariya (noble) path leading to the cessation of suffering.

Buddha's Eightfold Path consists of 1) right understanding; 2) right thinking; 3) right speech; 4) right conduct; 5) right livelihood; 6) right effort; 7) right mindfulness; 8) right concentration.

Buddhism is not a single monolithic religion. Many of its supporters have combined the teachings of Buddha with local religious rituals, beliefs and customs.

After the Buddha's death, splits occurred. There are now three main systems of thought within Buddhism, which are geographically and philosophically separate. Each tradition in turn has many sects. The three main Buddhists groups are Southern Buddhism (know as Theravada Buddhism), Eastern Buddhism and Northern Buddhism. Southern Buddhism has over 100 million followers, mainly in Burma, Cambodia, Laos, Sri Lanka and Thailand, and parts of Vietnam. It started in Sri Lanka when Buddhist missionaries arrived from India. They promoted the Vibhajjavada School (Separative Teaching). By the 15th century, this form of the religion reached almost its present extent. Concepts and practices include: Dana — thoughtful, ceremonial giving; Sila — accepting Buddhist teaching and following it in practice; refraining from killing, stealing, wrong behavior, use of drugs. On special days, three additional rules may be added, restricting adornment, entertainment and comfort; Karma — the balance of accumulated sin and merit, which will determine one's future in the present life, and the nature of the next life to come; The

Cosmos — consists of worlds grouped into clusters; clusters are grouped into galaxies, which are themselves grouped into super-galaxies. The universe also has many levels: four underworlds and 21 heavenly realms; Paritta — ritual chanting; Worship — of relics of a Buddha of items made by a Buddha, or of symbolic relics; Festivals — days of the full moon, and three other days during the lunar cycle are celebrated. There is a new year's festival, and celebrations tied to the agricultural year; Pilgrimages — particularly to Buddhist sites in Sri Lanka and India.

Eastern Buddhism is the predominant religion in China, Japan, Korea and Vietnam. Buddhism's Mahayana tradition entered China during the Han dynasty (206 BCE — 220 CE). It found initial acceptance there among the workers; later, it gradually penetrated the ruling class. Buddhism reached Japan in the 6th century.

Eastern Buddhism contains many distinct schools: T'ein-t'ai, Hua-yen, Pure Land teachings, and the Meditation school. They celebrate New Years, harvest festivals, and five anniversaries from the lives of Buddha and of the Bodhisattva Kuan-yin. They also engage in Dana, Sila, Chanting, Worship and Pilgrimage.

Northern Buddhism has around 10 million followers in parts of China, Mongolia, Russia and Tibet. It entered Tibet around 640 CE. Conflict with the native Tibetan religion of Bon caused it to go largely underground until its revival in the 11th century.

Ceremony and ritual are emphasized. They also engage in Dana, Sila, Chanting, Worship and Pilgrimage. They developed the practice of searching out a young child at the time of death of an important teacher. The child is believed to be the successor to the deceased teacher. They celebrate New Years, harvest festivals and anniversaries of five important events in the life of the Buddha.

CANON AND IMPORTANT TEXTS

Originally Buddhism existed as an oral tradition, but eventually was composed into two main language canons; the Pall and the Sanskrit. The Mahayana school following the Sanskrit and the Theravada school following the Pali canon.

From these two ancient sources arise the three most complete language canons of the modern era. The Pali Canon records the Buddha's teachings as accepted by the Theravada School; the Chinese Canon records the Buddha's teachings as accepted by the Mahayana School; and the Tibetan Canon records the Buddha's teachings as accepted by the Vajrayana School. The Dhammapada is the best known and most widely esteemed text in the Pali Tripitaka, the sacred scriptures of Theravada Buddhism. Composed in the ancient Pali language, this anthology of 423 verses uttered by the Buddha constitutes a perfect compendium of Buddha's teaching, comprising between its covers all the essential principles elaborated at length in the forty-odd volumes of the Pali Canon.

ISLAM

ORIGIN OF ISLAM

Islam was founded in 622 CE by Muhammad the Prophet. He lived from about 570 CE to 632 CE.

Many of the followers of Islam believe that Islam existed before Muhammad was born, the origins of Islam date back
to the creation of the world and Muhammad was the last of a series of Prophets.

Followers of Islam are called Muslims. Muslim is an Arabic word that refers to a person who submits himself or herself to the Will of God. "Allah" is an Arabic word, which means "the One True God".

ABOUT MUHAMMAD

Muhammad was born around 570 CE in the city of Mecca in Arabia.

While Muhammad was still young, he was sent into the desert to be raised by a foster family. This was a common practice at the time. He was orphaned at the age of six and brought up by his uncle. As a child, he worked as a shepherd and was taken on a caravan to Syria by his uncle. Later, as a youth, he was employed as a camel driver on the trade routes between Syria and Arabia. Muhammad later managed caravans on behalf of merchants. He met people of different religious beliefs on his travels, and was able to observe and learn about Judaism, Christianity and the indigenous Pagan religions.

At 25, Muhammad married a widow named Khadija, a noble lady of the Quraish tribe, who was involved in trade and got him involved in it as well. After marriage, he was able to spend more time on meditation. At the age of 40 (610 CE), he was visited in Mecca by the angel Gabriel. He developed the conviction that he had been ordained a Prophet and given the task of converting his countrymen from their pagan, polytheistic beliefs and what he regarded as moral decadence, idolatry, hedonism and materialism.

He met considerable opposition to his teachings. In 622 CE he moved north to Medina due to increasing persecution. The trek is known as the hegira. Here he was disappointed by the rejection of his message to the Jews. Through religious discussion, persuasion, military activity and political negotiation, Muhammad became the most powerful leader in Arabia, and Islam was firmly established throughout the area.

Muhammad died in 632 CE and it was left to his followers to carry on the traditions he had begun.

ABOUT ISLAM

By 750 CE, Islam had expanded to China, India, along the Southern shore of the Mediterranean and into Spain. By 1550
they had reached Vienna. Wars resulted, expelling Muslims from Spain and Europe. Since their trading routes were mostly over land, they did not develop an extensive sea trade (as for example the English and Spaniards). As a result, the Old World occupation of North America was left to Christians.

Islam believers are currently concentrated from the West Coast of Africa to the Philippines. In Africa, in particular, they are increasing in numbers, largely at the expense of Christianity.

Many do not look upon Islam as a new religion. They feel that it is in reality the faith taught by the ancient Prophets, Abraham, David, Moses and Jesus. Muhammad's role as the last of the Prophets was to formalize and clarify the faith and to purify it by removing foreign ideas that had been added in error.

IMPORTANT TEXTS

There are two main texts consulted by Muslims: The Qur'an and the Hadith. The Qur'an are the words of God. Muslims believe that it was revealed to Muhammad by the angel Gabriel. This was originally in oral and written form; they were later assembled into a single book. The Hadith, are collections of the sayings of Muhammad. They are regarded as the Sunnah (lived example) of Muhammad. However, the writings are not regarded as having the same status as the Holy Qur'an.

ISLAMIC BELIEFS

Islam considers six fundamental beliefs to be the foundation of their faith: 1) A single, indivisible God. (God, the creator, is just, omnipotent and merciful. "Allah" is often used to refer to God; it is the Arabic word for God.); 2) The angels; 3) The divine scriptures, which include the Torah, the Psalms, the rest of the Bible, (as they were originally revealed) and the Qur'an (which is composed of God's words, dictated by the angel Gabriel to Muhammad); 4) The Messengers of God, including Adam, Noah, Abraham, Moses, David, Jesus and Muhammad — the last prophet. Muhammad's message is considered the final, universal message for all of humanity; 5) The Day of Judgment when people will be judged on the basis of their deeds while on earth, and will either attain reward of Heaven or punishment in Hell. They do not believe that Jesus or any other individual can atone for another person's sin. Hell is where unbelievers and sinners spend eternity. Paradise is a place of physical and spiritual pleasure where the sinless go after death; 6) The supremacy of God's will. Other Common beliefs; 7) Belief in the existence of Satan who drives people to sin; 8) That Muslims who sincerely repent and submit to God return to a state of sinlessness; 9) Total and absolute rejection of racism. All people are considered children of Adam; 10) Avoid the use of alcohol, other drugs, eating of pork, etc; 11) Avoid gambling; 12) That Jesus is a prophet, born of the Virgin Mary. They regard the Christian concept of the deity of Jesus to be blasphemous; they view God is one and indivisible; God did not have a son; 13) That Jesus was not executed on the cross.

UNDERSTANDING OF JESUS, WITHIN ISLAM AND CHRISTIANITY

Traditional Christians and Muslims have certain beliefs in common concerning Jesus. They both accept that his birth was miraculous, he was the Messiah, he cured people of illness and he restored dead people to life.

Muslims, however, differ from Christians in a number of major areas. They do not believe: In original sin (that everyone inherits a sinful nature because of Adam and Eve's transgression), that Jesus was killed during a crucifixion. Muslims believe that he escaped being executed, and later reappeared to his disciples without having first died, that Jesus was resurrected (or resurrected himself) around 30 AD, and Salvation is dependent either upon belief in the resurrection of Jesus (as in Paul's writings) or belief that Jesus is the Son of God (as in the Gospel of John).

SCHOOLS WITHIN ISLAM

There are different schools of practice within Islam. The main divisions are Sunni Muslims, Shiite Muslims and Sufism. The Sunni Muslims are followers of the Hanifa, Shafi, Hanibal and Malik schools. They constitute a 90% majority of the believers, and are considered to be mainstream traditionalists. They have been able to adapt to a variety of national cultures, while following their three sources of law: the Koran, Hadith and consensus of Muslims. The Shiite Muslims are followers of the Jafri School who make up a small minority of Islam. They split from the Sunnis over a dispute about the successor to Muhammad. Their leaders promote a strict interpretation of the Koran and close adherents to its teachings. They believe in 12 heavenly Imams (perfect teachers) who led the Shiites in succession. Shiites believe that the 12th lmam, the Mahdi (guided one), never died but went into hiding for the right time to reappear and guide humans towards justice and peace. Sufism is a mystic tradition in which followers seek inner knowledge directly from God through meditation and ritual and dancing. They developed in the late 10th century as a (ascetic, practicing strict self-denial, severe) reaction to the formalism and laws of the Koran. There are Sufis from both the Sunni and Shiite groups. They incorporated ideas from Neoplatonism, Buddhism, and Christianity. They emphasize personal union with the divine.

Islam does not have denominational mosques. Members are welcome to attend any mosque in any land.

JUDAISM

Judaism is one of four Abramic religions — faiths that recognize Abraham, a Hebrew chieftain, originally from the Babylonian city of Ui, as a Patriarch. The others are Christianity, Islam and Baha'i World Faith. Although Jews comprise only about 0.2% of the human race, Jewish influence on the world has been vast — far more than their numbers would indicate. Jews believe that around 2000 BC the God of the ancient Israelites established a divine covenant with Abraham. The book of Genesis describes the events surrounding the lives of the three patriarchs: Abraham, Isaac, and Jacob. (Joseph, who is recognized as a fourth patriarch by Christians is not considered one by Jews). Moses was the next leader of the ancient Israelites. He led his people out of captivity in Egypt, and received the Law from God. Joshua later led them into the Promised Land where Samuel established the Israelite kingdom with Saul as its first king. King David established Jerusalem and King Solomon built the first temple there.

Four major religious sects had formed by the 1st century CE: the Basusim, Essenes, Pharisees and Sadducees. Many anticipated the arrival of the Messiah who would drive the Roman invaders out and restore independence. Christianity was established initially as a Jewish sect, centered in Jerusalem. Paul broke with this tradition and spread the religion to the Gentiles (non-Jews). Many mini-revolts led to the destruction of Jerusalem and its temple in 70 CE. The Jewish Christians were wiped out or scattered at this time. The movement by Paul flourished and quickly evolved into the religion of Christianity. Jews were scattered throughout the known world. Their religion was no longer centered in Jerusalem. Centuries elapsed with persecution between Christians and Jews.

The Zionist movement was a response within all Jewish tradition to centuries of Christian persecution. Their initial goal was to create a Jewish homeland in Palestine. The state of Israel was formed in 1948.

There are currently about 18 million Jews throughout

the world. They are mainly concentrated in North America (about 7 million) and Israel (about 4.5 million).

SACRED TEXTS

The Tanakh corresponds to the Jewish Scriptures, (often referred to as the Old Testament by Christians). It is composed of three groups of books: 1) Torah (aka Pentateuch): Genesis, Exodus, Leviticus, Numbers and Deuteronomy; 2) Nevium: Joshua, Judges, Samuel II, Kings II, Isaiah, Jeremiah, Ezekiel, Hosea, Joel, Amos, Obadiah, Jonah, Micah, Nahum, Habakkuk, Zephaniah, Haggai, Zachariah, Malachilsaiah, Amos; and 3) Ketuvim: the "Writings" including Psalms, Proverbs, Job, Song of Songs, Ecclesiasters, Ruth, Esther, Lamentations, Daniel, Ezra, Nehemiah, Chronicles II.

The Talmud contains stories, laws, medical knowledge, debates about moral choices, etc. It is composed of material which comes mainly from two sources: 1) the Mishnah, 6 "orders" containing hundreds of chapters, including series of laws from the Hebrew Scriptures. It was compiled about 200 CE and 2) the Gemara (one Babylonian and one Palestinian) is encyclopedic in scope. It includes comments from hundreds of Rabbis from 200-500 CE, explaining the Mishnah with additional historical, religious, legal and sociological material.

JEWISH BELIEFS

Jews believe God is the creator who alone is to be worshipped as absolute ruler of the universe. The Torah (the first five books of the Hebrew Bible) was revealed to Moses by God and cannot be changed though God does communicate with the Jewish people through prophets. God monitors the activities of humans, rewarding individuals for good deeds and punishes evil. Jews generally consider actions and behavior to be of primary importance; beliefs come out of actions. Jews believe in the inherent goodness of the world and its inhabitants as creations of God and do not require a savior to save them from original sin. They believe they are God's chosen people and that the Messiah will arrive in the future, gather them into Israel, there will be a general resurrection of the dead, and the Jerusalem Temple destroyed in 70 CE will be rebuilt.

JEWISH PRACTICES

Jews observe the Sabbath as a day of rest, starting at sundown on Friday evening. They believe in strict discipline, according to the Law, which governs all areas of life. Regular attendance by Jewish males at their Synagogue is required. Celebration of annual festivals include: Passover (held each Spring to recall the Jews' deliverance out of slavery in Egypt around 1300 BCE), Rosh Hashanah (Jewish New Year, is the anniversary of the completion of creation, about 5760 years ago; held in the fall), Yom Kippur (Day of Atonement, fasting and penitence), Sukkoth (eight day harvest festival; a time of thanksgiving), Hanukkah (eight day feast of dedication. It recalls the war fought by the Maccabees in the cause of religious freedom; observed in December), Purim (recalls the defeat by Queen Esther of the plan to slaughter all of the Persian Jews, around 400 BCE), and Shavout (recalls God's revelation of the Torah to the Jewish people; held in late May or early June).

JEWISH MOVEMENTS

There are four main forms of Judaism today: 1) Conservative Judaism — this began in the mid-nineteenth century as a reaction against the Reform movement. It is a mainline movement midway between Reform and Orthodox. 2) Orthodox Judaism — this is the oldest, most conservative, and most diverse form of Judaism. They attempt to follow the original form of Judaism as they view it to be. They look upon every word in their sacred texts as being divinely inspired. 3) Reconstructionist Judaism — this is a new, small, liberal movement started by Mordecai Kaplan as an attempt to unify and revitalize the religion. They reject the concept that Jews are a uniquely favored and chosen people. 4) Reform Judaism — they are a liberal group, followed by many North American Jews. The movement started in the 1790's in Germany. They follow the ethical laws of Judaism, but leave up to the individual the decision whether to follow or ignore the dietary and other traditional laws. They use modern forms of worship. There are many female rabbis in the reform congregations.

SIKHISM

The Sikh faith was founded around 1500 CE by Shri Guru Nanak Dev Ji who lived from 1469 to 1539 CE, in the Punjab area, now Pakistan. He began preaching the way to enlightenment and God after receiving a vision. After his death a series of nine Gurus (regarded as the reincarnations of Guru Nanak) led the movement until 1704. At the time these functions passed to the Panth and the holy text. The tenth Guru, Gobind Singh (1666 CE — 1708 CE), revised this text, the Shri Guru Granth Sahib (also known as the Adi Granth) in 1704. It consists of over 6,000 hymns and writings of the first 10 Gurus, along with texts from different Muslim and Hindu saints. The holy text is considered the 11th and final Guru.

Sikh believe in a single formless God with many names, who can be known through meditation. Sikhs pray many times each day and are prohibited from worshipping idols or icons. They believe in samsara, karma, and reincarnation as Hindus do but reject the caste system. They believe that everyone has equal status in the eyes of God. During the 18th century, there were a number of attempts to prepare an accurate portrayal of Sikh customs. Sikh scholars and theologians started in 1931 to prepare the Reht Maryada — the Sikh code of conduct and conventions. This has successfully achieved a high level of uniformity in the religious and social practices of Sikhism throughout the world. It contains 27 articles. Article I defines who is a Sikh: "Any human being who faithfully believes in: 1) One immortal Being, 2) Ten Gurus, from Guru Nanak Dev to Guru Gobind Singh, 3) The Guru Granth Sahib, 4) The utterances and teachings of the ten Gurus and 5) The baptism bequeathed by the tenth Guru, and who does not owe allegiance to any other religion, is a Sikh."

Sikhs number around 22.5 million worldwide. Most live in the Pakistan.

BAHA'I FAITH

The Baha'i faith is the youngest of the world's main religions. The Baha'i religion originally grew out of Babism, which was founded by Mirza Ali Muhammad of Shiraz in Iran. Muhammad predicted that a new prophet from God would appear and overturn old beliefs and customs, ushering in a new era; these beliefs originated within the Shiite sect of Islam, which believed in the forthcoming return of the 12th Imam (successor of Muhammad), who would renew religion and guide the faithful.

In 1844 Mirza Ali Muhammad began proclaiming his beliefs and took on the title of the "Bab" ("Gateway"), and on May 23, 1844, he announced "The Declaration of Bab".

The "Bab's" teachings spread throughout Iran, provoking strong resistance from both the Shiite Muslim clergy and the government. "The Bab was arrested, incarcerated and executed in 1850. There were executions of 20,000 Babi followers as well.

TRANSITION TO BAHAI

One of the Babs's earliest disciples and strongest exponents was Mirza Hoseyn Ali Nun (1817-1892). Mirza Hoseyn was a member of the Shiite branch of Islam. After the Bab's execution Mirza Hoseyn joined Mirza Yahya (his own half brother) and the Bab's spiritual heir, in directing the Babi movement. Mirza Yahya later was discredited and Mirza Hoseyn, who had assumed the name of Baha Ullah, was arrested in 1852 and jailed in Tehran, Iran. It was during his incarceration that he felt he was the prophet that Bab had predicted.

A year later he was released and exiled to Baghdad, where his leadership revived the Babi community.

On April 21, 1863, Baha UIlah declared that he was the messenger of God foretold by the Bab. An overwhelming majority of the Babis acknowledged his claim and thus became known as Baha'is. Baha Ullah was subsequently confined by The Ottoman government in Turkey, and then moved to the prison city of Acre, Palestine for the last 22 years of his life. Before his death in 1892, he appointed his eldest son, Abd ol-Baha (1844-1921) as his successor. Abd ol-Baha spread the movement to North America (1893), Europe, and other continents. He appointed his eldest grandson, Shoghi Effendi Rabbani (1897-1957) as his successor.

The Baha'i faith underwent a rapid expansion in the early 1960's, and by the end of the 20th century had a following of about 6 million members worldwide.

BELIEFS

The followers believe that God has sent nine great prophets to mankind through whom the Holy Spirit has revealed the "Word of God." (The prophets are Adam, Abraham, Moses, Krishna, Zoroaster, Buddha, Jesus Christ, Muhammad, The Bab and Baha UIIah. They believe that God will continue to send prophets into the world. This has given rise to the major world religions. Although these religions arose from the teachings of the prophets of one God, Bahai's do not believe they are the same. The differences in the teachings of each prophet are due to the needs of the society they came to help and what mankind was ready to have revealed to it. Baha'i beliefs promote gender and race equality, freedom of expression and assembly, world peace and world government. They believe that a single world government led by Baha'is will be established at some point in the future. The faith does not attempt to preserve the past but does embrace the findings of science. Baha'is believe that every person has an immortal soul, which cannot die but is freed to travel through the spirit world after death.

SACRED TEXTS

Baha'i scripture comprises the writings from the "Bab", Baha Ultah, and Abdu'l Baha. Baha Ullah's most common works are The Most Holy Book, The Book of Certitude, Gleanings from the Writings of Baha UIIah, The Hidden Words and The Seven Valleys. There are many other books of Baha'i scripture.

CONFUCIANISM

K'ung Fu Tzu, best known by the Latin form of his name, Confucius, was born in 551 BCE in the state of Lu (modern day Shantung Province, China). Confucius lived in during the Chou dynasty, an era of political violence and social disintegration. He is believed to have worked as a minor civil servant and teacher; eventually as minister of justice in the state of Lu. He traveled through many states of China, giving advice to its rulers and teaching.

Confucius was said to have attracted 3,000 students, of whom 72 were close disciples. His teachings and writings dealt with individual morality and ethics, and the proper exercise of political power by the rulers. Confucius was not the founder of Confucianism in the sense that Buddha was the founder of Buddhism and Jesus Christ of Christianity. Rather, Confucius considered himself a transmitter who consciously tried to reanimate the old in order to attain the new. There are approximately 6 million Confucians in the world; majority are throughout China and Asia.

BELIEFS AND PRACTICES

Confucian ethical teachings include the following values: 1) Li: includes ritual, propriety, etiquette; 2) Hsiao: love among family members; 3) Yi: righteousness; 4) Xin: honesty and trustworthiness; 5) Jen: benevolence towards others — the highest Confucian virtue; 6) Chung: loyalty to the state.

Unlike most religions, Confucianism is primarily an ethical system with rituals at important times during one's lifetime. The most important periods recognized in the Confucian tradition are birth, reaching maturity, marriage and death.

SCHOOLS OF CONFUCIANISM

There are six schools of Confucianism: Han Confucianism, Neo-Confucianism, Contemporary Neo-Confucianism, Korean Confucianism, Japanese Confucianism and Singapore Confucianism.

SACRED TEXTS

    Chu Hsi (1130-1200 CE) assembled the following books during the Sung dynasty: The Si Shu or Four Books, which are 1) The Lun Yu or the Analects of Confucius; 2) The Chung Yung or the Doctrine of the Mean; 3) The Ta Hsueh or the Great Learning; 4) The Meng Tzu the writings of Meng Tzu (371-289 BCE); a philosopher who, like Confucius, traveled from state to state conversing with the government rulers. The Wu Jing or Five Classics, which are 1) Shu Ching or Classic of History: writings and speeches from ancient Chinese rulers; 2) The Shih Ching or Classic of Odes: 300 poems and songs; 3) The I Ching or Classic of changes: the description of a divintory system involving 64 hexagrams; 4) The Ch'un Ch'iu or Spring and Autumn Annuals: a history of the state of Lu from 722 to 484 BCE; 5) The Li Ching or Classic of Rites: a group of three books on the Li (the rites of correct and appropriate behavior).

JANISM

Legend records show Rishabhadeva was the first Thirthankara, or Prophet of Jainism. Rishabhadeva is thought to have lived around 1500 BCE. Vardhamana Mahavira (born in 599 BCE) through self-example and his lifetime teachings revived the religion and made it popular in India. He attained enlightenment after 13 years of deprivation and committed the act of salekhana, (fasting to death) in 527 BCE. Mahavira is regarded by Jains as the last of the 24 Thirthankaras, or Prophets of Jainism.

Jainism has many similarities to Hinduism and Buddhism, which developed, in the same part of the world. They believe in karma and reincarnation as do Hindus but they believe that enlightenment and liberation from this cycle can only be achieved through asceticism. Jains follow fruititarianism. This is the practice of only eating that, which will not kill the plant, or animal from which it is taken. They also practice akimsa, (non-violence), because any act of violence against a living thing creates negative karma, which will adversely affect one's next life.

One of the most important activities of the Prophets of Jainism was the search for an understanding of the universe.

According to Jainism there are three principle regions of the universe. The first region is that of several heavens. The highest level is that of the liberated souls know as the Realm of the Jinas. The middle level is the heaven of the gods where different types of deities exist. One of the realms is known by humans and is known as Jambudvipa (the continent of the rose-apple tree). In this realm humans may find rewards for religious pursuits and that deliverance may be possible. The third region in the Jain universe are the eight hells with each, in descending order, more horrible than the last. Existence in any of these hells is not permanent; a person may be born again into a new form once he or she has been sufficiently punished. The Jain vision of hell is one that gets progressively colder with each descent into the lower levels.

There are two groups of Jains: The Digambaras — their

monks carry asceticism to the point of rejecting even clothing, even when they appear in public; and The Shvetambaras — their monks wear simple white robes. The followers are permitted to wear clothes of any color.

There are around 4 million Jains; almost entirely located in India.

SHINTO

The indigenous religious beliefs and practices of Japan are termed Shinto. Shinto came into use in order to distinguish indigenous Japanese beliefs from Buddhism, which had been introduced into Japan in the 6th century CE. Shinto is closely tied to nature, which recognized the existence of various "Kami" (translated as "god" or "gods"). Shinto creation stories and mythology tell of the history and lives of the first two deities, Izanagi and Izanami, a divine couple, who gave birth to the Japanese islands. Their children became the deities of the various Japanese clans. One of their daughters, Amaterasu (Sun Goddess), is the ancestress of the Imperial Family and is regarded as the chief deity. A descendant of Amaterasu, Jimmu, is said to have become the first emperor of Japan. Followers of Shinto desire peace and believe all human life is sacred. They revere "musuhi", the Kami's creative and harmonizing powers, and aspire to have "makoto", sincerity or true heart. Morality is based upon that which is of benefit to the group.

There are four main forms of Shinto, all closely inter-related. Koshitsu Shinto (The Shinto of the Imperial House) involves rituals performed by the emperor, who the Japanese constitution defines to be the "symbol of the state and of the unity of the people." The most important ritual is Niinamesai, which makes an offering to the deities of the first fruits of each year's grain harvest. Male and female clergy assist the emperor in the performance of these rites. Shrine Shinto (Jinja Shinto) is largest Shinto group. It was the original form of the religion; dating back to the beginning of Japanese history. Shrine Shinto is a general term for all the rites and other activities performed by a local community or a kin community mainly in a building called Jinja (or a shrine). Folk Shinto (Minzoku Shinto) closely tied to Shrine Shinto, and is centered on the veneration of small roadside images, with a particular focus on agricultural rituals and practices. Sect Shinto (Kyoha Shinto) consists of 13 sects, which were founded by individuals since the start of the 19th century. Each sect has its own beliefs and doctrines.

Most emphasize worship of their own central deity.

Unlike most other religions, Shinto has no real founder, no written scriptures, no body of religious law, and only a very loosely organized priesthood. There are, however, some texts that stand out and are commonly read among practitioners: the Kojiki (The Record of Ancient Matters, 712 CE), and the Nihon Shoki (Chronicles of Japan, 720 CE).

Shinto in itself has no defining morality of its own. Essentially, in the Shinto worldview, the world is good, people are good, and there is harmony — which is threatened by evil spirits, who must be dispelled and kept at bay.

There are "Four Affirmations" in Shinto: 1) Tradition and family — the family is the main mechanism by which traditions are preserved. 2) Love of nature — nature is sacred and natural objects are to be worshipped as sacred spirits. 3) Physical cleanliness — they must take baths, wash their hands, and rinse their mouth often. 4) "Matsuri" — festival which honors the spirits.

Estimates of followers of Shinto are in the range 2.8-3.2 million with essentially all the followers of Shinto are Japanese.

TAOISM

Taoism was founded by Lao-Tse (604-531 BCE) a contemporary of Confucius in China. Taoism began as a combination of psychology and philosophy, which Lao-Tse hoped, would help end the constant feudal warfare and other conflicts that disrupted society during his lifetime. His writings, the Tao-te-Ching, describe the nature of life, the way to peace and how a ruler should lead his life.

Religious Taoism was started when Chiang Ling claimed that he had received a revelation from Lao-Tse, which instructed him to implement Lao-Tse's "orthodox and sole doctrine of the authority of the covenant". Upon his death, it is said Chiang Ling ascended to Heaven where he earned the title Heavenly Master.

After he obtained this title, a succession of followers who were also called Heavenly Masters founded an independent organization to instruct the faithful on the works of Lao-Tse.

In about 215 CE Chiang Ling's grandson was the first to have Taoism recognized as an organized religion. Religious Taoism became a state religion in China in 440 CE. Tao, roughly translated as a path, is a force which flows through all life and is the first cause of everything. The goal of everyone is to become one with the Tao. Tai Chi, a technique of exercise using slow deliberate movements, is used to balance the flow of energy or "chi" within the body. People should develop virtue and seek compassion, moderation and humility. One should plan any action in advance and achieve it through minimal action. Yin (dark side) and Yang (light side) symbolize pairs of opposites, which are seen through the universe, such as good and evil, light and dark, male and female. The impact of human civilization upset the balance of Yin and Yang. Taoists believe that people are by nature, good, and that one should be kind to others simply because such treatment will be reciprocated.

Taoism currently has about 20 million followers, and is primarily centered in Taiwan.

CHRISTIANITY

INTRODUCTION AND HISTORY

Christianity emerged from Judaism in the first century CE. The Christian religion follows the teachings of Yeshua of Nazareth. Later, Pauline Christians gave him the title of Jesus Christ (Jesus is the Greek version of Yeshua; Christ means Messiah, or the anointed one. He was a traveling Jewish preacher who was born around 4 to 7 BCE.

Most Fundamentalist and Evangelical Christians believe that his mother, Mary was a virgin when he was conceived; her pregnancy was caused by the Holy Spirit, and did not result from sexual intercourse. He was raised by his Jewish family of origin in the city of Nazareth in the Galilee. Jesus was the oldest child in the family, having four brothers and at least two sisters.

At the age of about 30, around 26 CE he was baptized by John the Baptist, a relative of Jesus, a Jewish prophet, and probably a member of the Essences. The Essences were the smallest of the four main Jewish religious political groups active in Jerusalem at the time; the others being the Pharisees, Sadducees, and Zealots. Jesus became a traveling preacher whose message found an enthusiastic audience. He collected a group of followers (half men, half women) during his ministry of which about 10 is fully described in the Christian Scriptures (New Testament).

During this period, Palestine was very unstable politically; it had been under severe Roman oppression for decades. Many Jews expressed belief in a coming Messiah (anointed one) who would lead them to a military victory over the occupation forces and reign as king. This would be follow by the Reign of God on earth. Zealots were actively promoting the overthrow of the Romans.

Running afoul of the occupation army, Jesus is recorded in the Christian Scriptures (New Testament) as being betrayed by Judas, one of his followers. He was executed in Jerusalem, possibly during the springtime, around 30 CE by the Roman authorities. The Christian Scriptures describe that, after his death, Jesus was resurrected by God (or resurrected himself). He visited with his followers for a few weeks (or for a single day, according to Luke) and then ascended to Heaven. Many of his followers expected that he would return shortly and initiate the Kingdom of God on earth.

After Jesus' death, the followers of Jesus formed the Jewish Christian movement, centered in Jerusalem, under the leadership of James, one of Jesus' brothers. They regarded themselves as a reform movement within Judaism; they viewed Jesus as a prophet and rabbi, but not as a deity. They organized a synagogue, continued to sacrifice animals at the Jerusalem Temple, circumcised their male children, observed the Jewish holy days, and followed Jewish Kosher dietary laws and practiced the teachings of Jesus as they interpreted them to be.

Saul of Tarsus, a Greek Jew and originally a persecutor of the Jewish Christians, reported having a vision of the risen Christ (He believed he had received instructions directly from Jesus to devote the rest of his life to spreading the gospel to the Gentiles).

To recognize this event, he changed his name to Paul. Paul became the greatest theologian of the early Christian movement; creating a new Christian movement: Pauline Christianity. He included the concept of Jesus as "The Word", as god-man, the savior of humanity, the product of a virgin birth who was executed, resurrected and ascended into heaven. Paul abandoned most of the Laws of Moses and rejected many of the Jewish behavioral rules that Jesus and his disciples had followed during his ministry. Paul taught that God had unilaterally abrogated his covenants with the Jews and transferred them to the Pauline Christian groups.

Paul went on a series of missionary journeys around the eastern Mediterranean and attracted many Gentiles (non-Jews) to his movement. He had many co-workers, both male and female. Paul organized churches in many of the urban centers, in competition with Greek Paganism, Mithraism, Mystery

Religions, Judaism, competing Christian movements, and other religions. His letters record how he and his movement were in continual theological conflict with the Jewish Christian movement centered in Jerusalem, and with Gnostic Christians. For example, Paul believed circumcision was necessary and that male converts were not required to follow Jewish laws. The Jewish Christian movement questioned Paul's claim to be an apostle, since he had never met Jesus in real life. However, Paul's outstanding oratory skills and organizing abilities made it possible to build a network of Christian churches that eventually grew to cover almost all of the Western World. By the time that Jesus' original followers (now called Apostles) died, most of the Christians in the world were Gentiles (non-Jews).

Christian groups typically met in the homes of individuals. Leaders of these individual congregations were both men and women; and were often called bishops, elders or pastors. There was no central authority, no dedicated church buildings or cathedrals.

Eventually, Paul, Peter and a number of other Apostles ran afoul of the Roman Empire, were arrested and executed around 65 CE. Paul's churches survived his death and flourished.

In 70 CE, the Romans destroyed the Jerusalem Temple and the rest of Jerusalem. Many Jews were killed; others fled Palestine. After an unsuccessful Jewish uprising between 132-135 CE the Roman Army drove the Jews from Palestine. The Nazoreans were thus dispersed throughout the Roman Empire. This severely weakened the movement. The Jewish Christian movement (after having a brief resurgence in the 2nd century CE) gradually disappeared. The Pauline Christian movement grew to become the established church. It started an unofficial canon of writings which were later to become the Christian Scriptures (New Testament). From the many Christian gospels and letters (Epistles) they chose a few that more or less matched the theology of the developing church.

Admittance of the Gospel of John into the official canon had to overcome a great deal of resistance; many in the church that it had too much Gnostic content. The canon accepted: Four gospels, written by unknown authors, but attributed to Matthew, Mark, Luke and John; Acts of the Apostles, apparently written by the same author who wrote Luke; Thirteen Pauline Epistles — letters which claim that they were written by Paul. Religious liberals accept that seven were written by Paul, one may have been written by him, and five were by unknown authors — mostly from the second century many decades after Paul's death; eight general Epistles — James, John, Peter, Hebrews and Jude — all by anonymous authors with the possible exception of Hebrews which may have been written by Priscilla; Revelation, a book about the end of the world.

The third main group within the middle to late first century CE was Gnostic Christianity. Gnostic Christianity consisted of many separate groups with no appreciable central organization. Gnosticism is a philosophical and religious movement with roots in pre-Christian times. Gnostics combined elements taken from Judaism, other Christian movements, and from Pagan religions from the Middle East and Asia.

Some worked within existing congregations of the Jewish Christians and within the churches by Paul and his followers. They had many novel concepts about the nature of Jesus and God. They claimed to have secret knowledge about God, humanity and the rest of the universe of which the general population was unaware.

They had tolerance of different religious beliefs within and outside of Gnosticism and did not discriminate against women.

However, due to the increasing popularity and persecution by Pauline Christians, Gnostic Christianity went into a steep decline, and ceased being a significant force by the 6th century.

Between 170 to 325 CE many religious movements were active in the Roman Empire: Christianity, Greek and Roman Pagan religions, Judaism, Mithraism and various secret mystery religions.

Many points of conflict developed between the Roman authorities about the growing Christian movement.

Some of the conflicts that most Christians were opposed to were: each adult was expected to sponsor a sacrifice in the Roman Temple once per year, adults were expected to acknowledge Caesar as the Son of God and Savior, and that the state refused marriage between a free person and a slave. As a result of these conflicts Christians were frequently persecuted in various parts of the Empire.

In 323 CE the year of Christian persecution came to an end. Emperor Constantine issued the Edict of Milan, which formally established freedom and toleration of all religions, including Christianity.

However, there was no person or group who could speak for the entire church, no one person who had the authority to decide matters of beliefs and practices. Such matters could only be determined by councils at which all the available bishops would debate and attempt to resolve their differences. It was only in 325 CE that bishops from throughout the Christian movement would be able to meet at the Council of Nicea and attempt to resolve differences in Christian beliefs. The Bishops attempted to resolve a major conflict facing the early church: the relationship between Jesus and God. The church recognized the Hebrew Scriptures (Old Testament), which described God in strictly monotheistic terms, but there were conflicting theories about the deity of Jesus: One group led by Anus believed that Jesus and God were separate and different. They believed that Jesus was created by God and therefore at one point did not exist and that he was not divine. The other group led by Athansasius believed that Jesus was one with God, same substance as God the Father and external. After voting in favor of Athanasius, the dissenting bishops were offered two options: to sign the settlement at Nicea or be exiled. The bishops produced the Nicene Creed, which declared that Jesus Christ was "of one substance with the Father." This did not immediately settle the question of the divinity of Christ; many bishops and churches refused to believe in the council's decision for decades.

Emperor Constantine in 330 CE, decided to build a "New Rome" which he called Constantinople. It became the center of the largely Christian empire. By this time, the church had evolved from a small, scattering of congregations to a geographically widespread church under the authority of many bishops.

The bishop granted to the bishop of Alexandria (in Egypt) authority over the eastern half of the empire, and to the bishop of Rome the western portion of the empire.

The Emperor Theodosian issued a series of decrees in the years 341-391 CE. Basically the order was to "suppress all rival religions, order the closing of the temples, and to impose fines, confiscation, imprisonment or death upon any who cling to the older (Pagan) religions". The period of relative religious tolerance in the Rome Empire ended. Christianity and Judaism became the only permitted religions. The Church used the power of the state to begin programs to oppress, exile or exterminate both Pagans and Gnostic Christians.

During the next two or three hundred years several church councils met to resolve conflicts between the various congregations and impose new decrees.

The Roman Empire recognized Pauline Christianity as a valid religion in 313 CE. Later in that century, it became the official religion of the Empire.

Authority within the church was centering on the Bishop of Rome in the west and the Patriarch of Constantinople in the east. Divisions between the two power centers in the Christian church gradually intensified. The next few centuries the Roman Catholic Church and the Eastern Orthodox Church became increasingly remote from each other until a formal split occurred in 1054 CE. Each contends that it more correctly maintains the tradition of the early church and that the other has deviated. Roman Catholic Christians prefer to themselves as "catholic" which means "universal", and maintain that they are also orthodox. Eastern Orthodox Christians often refer to themselves simply as "orthodox" which means, "right worship", and also call themselves catholic. Originally the schism the split was between the East and West, but today both have congregations all over the world.

In 1517, Martin Luther, a Christian monk from Germany, said that the Roman Catholic Church was corrupt and that it should be reformed. Luther also argued that a reformation was need of other things such as the language the Bible was produced in was Latin, but most people couldn't read Latin; and the selling of forgiveness, this was considered immoral by Luther but had been standard practice by some monks and priests for years. The ideas behind the Protestant Reformation were simple. The church should be changed, or reformed, so that it was less greedy, fairer and accessible to all people, not just the rich and well educated.

A split followed, producing the Protestant Reformation and a series of religious wars, which decimated Western Europe. Protestantism subsequently split into many movements which themselves split into families of denominations.

The result was the thousands of individual Protestant denominations and sects that we observe today.

ZOROASTRIANISM

Zoroastrianism is one of the oldest religions still in existence and may have been the first monotheistic religion. Zoroastrianism's theology has had a great impact on Judaism, Christianity and other religions, in the beliefs surrounding God and Satan, the soul, heaven and hell, savior, resurrection, final judgment and more.

The religion was founded by Zarathustra sometime between 1500 and 1000 BCE (timeframe is based on his style of writing according to historians).

Zarathustra was born near the Oxus River in Persia modern day Iran. Legends say that his birth was predicted and that attempts were made by the forces of evil to kill him as a child.

According to tradition, Zarathustra's initial revelation came at the age of 30. While drawing water, Zarathustra had a shining vision. A being calling itself Vohu Manah ("Good Purpose") appeared to him and took him into the presence of Ahura Mazda. Zarathustra then received a revelation that Ahura Mazda was the single, eternal and moral creator God.

Zarathustra began preaching monotheism in a land which followed an aboriginal polytheistic religion. His preaching and teachings to his own people was rejected; Zarathustra joined a different tribe. Zarathustra and his message finally won the support of the prince, Vishtaspa, who was able to aggressively defend the growing new religion, its converts, and their territory.

Zoroastrianism became the state religion of various Persian empires until the 7th century CE.

Zoroastrianism became highly institutionalized, with a special class of priests (magi), many temples, and established rituals.

When Arabs, followers of Islam, invaded Persia in 650 CE, conversion to Islam was forced or highly encouraged, A small number of Zoroastrians fled to India were most are concentrated today.

The conditions of Zarathustra's death are uncertain,

and the exact means by which the religion institutionalized unknown. However, the faith found widespread support in the 6th century BCE during which tribes conquered and displaced one another.

The Zoroastrian holy book is called the Avesta. This includes the original words of their founder Zarathustra, preserved in a series of five hymns, called the Gathas. The later represent the core text of the religion. The Gathas are abstract sacred poetry, directed towards the worship of the One God, understanding of righteousness and cosmic order, promotion of social justice and individual choice between good and evil. The Gathas have a general and even universal vision. The Avesta was probably transmitted orally until the 9th century CE. At some later date (most historical scholars say many centuries later), the remaining parts of the Avestas were written. These deal with laws of ritual and practice, with the traditions of faith. The Zoroastrian community is sharply divided between those who would follow mostly or exclusively the teachings of the original Gathas, and those who believe that the later traditions are important and equally divinely inspired.

Zoroastrianism has become a small religion with about 140,000 members.

SACRED TEXTS OF THE
MAJOR RELIGIONS

BUDDHISM

Tripitaka (Pall Canon) - The Tripitaka (Pall Canon) is the earliest collection of Buddhist teachings and the only text recognized as canonical by Theravada Buddhists. The Tripitaka was handed down orally, then written down in the third century BCE According to Buddhist tradition, the contents of the Tripitaka were determined at the First Buddhist Council, shortly after the Buddha's death. As many as 500 of Buddha's disciples assembled and at the direction of Mahakashypa, Buddha's successor, the teachings of the Buddha were recited in full They were then verified by others who had also been present and organized into the Tripitaka.

Mahayana Sutras - Mahayana Buddhism reveres the Tripitaka as a sacred text, but adds it to the Sutras, which reflect Mahayana concepts. Most of the Mahayana Sutras, which number over two thousand, were written between 200 BCE and 200 CE, the period in which Mahayana Buddhism developed.

Tibetan Book of the Dead — The Tibetan Book of the Dead is the Tibetan text that is most well known to the West. Written by a Tibetan monk, the Book of the Dead describes in detail the stages of death from the Tibetan point of view.

HINDUISM

Hindu sacred texts fall into one of two categories: sruti ("heard") or smruti ("remembered"). Sruti scriptures are considered divinely inspired and fully authoritative for belief and practice, while smruti are recognized as the products of the minds of the great sages.

However, smruti texts often carry almost as much authority as sruti, and the religion of the older sruti texts bears little resemblance to modern Hinduism and is largely unknown to the average Hindu. But, the sruti are still held in very high regard and portions are still memorized for religious merit. The only texts regarded as sruti are the Vedas, which are the most sacred scriptures of Hinduism. The Vedas ("Books of Knowledge") are a collection of texts written in Sanskrit from about 1200 BCE to 100 CE. As sruti, the Vedas are regarded as the absolute authority for religious knowledge and a test of Hindu orthodoxy. Selections from the Vedas are still memorized and recited for religious merit today.

Smruti texts help sruti scriptures and make them meaningful to the general population. Despite their lesser authority, they are generally the most recent, the most beloved by the Hindu population, and the most representative of actual Hindu beliefs and practices. Smruti texts include the Itihasas (History or Epics), Puranas (Mythology), Dharma Shastras (Law Codes), Agamas and Tantras (Sectarian Scriptures), and Darshanas (Manuals of Philosophy).

ISLAM

There are two main sacred texts in Islam: the Qur'an and the Hadith. The Qur'an is the most sacred text, as it is believed to be the literal word of God as revealed to Muhammad. The Qur'an was put in writing shortly after Muhammad's death in 632 CE. The Hadith is a secondary text that records sayings of Muhammad and his followers. These two texts form the basis for all Islamic theology, practice and Islamic law.

The Judeo-Christian Bible is also respected as revelations from the true God, but Muslims believe the Bible to have been corrupted in transmission and translation.

JUDAISM

Tanakh — The Jewish sacred text is the Tanakh. It consists of the same books as the Christian Old Testament, although in a slightly different order and with other minor differences. Sometimes the word "Torah" is used to refer to the entire Tanakh or even the whole body of Jewish writings, but it technically means the first five books of the Tanakh.

SIKHISM

The ultimate source of authority and doctrine in Sikhism is the Guru Granth Sahib (the Sikh Holy Book) compiled in 1600 CE by the fifth Guru, Adi Granth.

TAOISM

Tao-te Ching — is the central text of both philosophical and religious Taoism. In English, its name is translated as Classic of the Way of Power. Scholars believe the text was compiled by Lao-tsu and other authors over a period of centuries. The date of its composition vary between the 8th century and 3rd century BCE. The oldest existing manuscript dates to about 200 BCE.

Chuang-tzu — The Chuang-tzu is named for its primary author, "Master Chuang" (c. 369-286 BCE). The Chuang-tzu focuses a great deal on the person of Lao-tzu, who is presented as one of Chuang-Tzu's teachers.

BAHA'I

Kitab-I-Aqbas — the Kitab-l-Aqbas (also known as The Most Holy Book) written by Mirza Hoseyn 'Au Nun, known as Bahaullah is the most holy text. This text forms the book of laws in the Baha'i Faith. The Kitab-l-Agbas was written in 1863 CE.

CHRISTIANITY

The Bible — The primary sacred text of Christianity is the Bible. The Christian Bible is made of two parts: the Old Testament, which is also identical to the Jewish Bible; and the New Testament, a collection of Christian writings that includes biographies of Jesus and the apostles, letters to new churches, and an apocalyptic work. The bible was written from about I 450 BCE to 100 CE. The Bible was written by many different authors writing in many different times and places.

Catholic and Orthodox bibles include the Apocrypha, while

most Protestant Bibles do not. The Aprocrypha is a group of 13 Jewish books written between the Old Testament and the New Testament.

CONFUCIANISM

Lun-yu (Analects) — The Lun-yu (Analects) are the most revered scripture in the Confucian tradition. It was probably compiled by the second generation of Confucius' disciples.

MORMONISM

Mormons recognize four main texts as divinely inspired and authoritative scripture. These are called the "Standard Works": 1) The Book of Mormon: Another Testament of Jesus Christ — The Book of Mormon was an English translation from the golden plates (Joseph Smith claims he discovered in 1823) that was first published in 1830. The Book of Mormon is a record of God's work and Christ's appearance among the ancient natives of North America; 2) The Christian Bible (King James translation); 3) The Doctrine and Covenants — a collection of revelations and inspired declarations composed of 138 revelations from God, 135 of which were recorded by Joseph Smith, plus one each by John Taylor, Brigham Young, and Joseph F. Smith. Two "Official declarations" which are more recent revelations. One was added in 1890 concerning polygamy; one was added in 1978 concerning the role of black persons in the Church; 4) The Pearl of Great Price, which is composed of two lost books of the Bible — the Book of Moses and the Book of Abraham; a translation of the Gospel of Matthew; Joseph Smith history and The Mormon 13 Articles of Faith.

SHINTO

Shinto does not have official scripture that can be compared to texts like the Bible or the Qur'an. But the Kojiki

(Records of Ancient Matters) and the Nihon shoki (Chronicles of Japan) are in a sense the sacred books of Shinto. They were written in 712 and 720 CE.

JAINISM

The sacred texts of Jainism are the teachings of the 24 Tirthankaras, those who gained omniscience. The texts are known as Agamas written in Prakrit and contain basic Jain doctrine, codes of practice, and narrative literature. They were written around 500 CE. (The sacred texts of the Jains are called Agamas. The texts were spoken orally for centuries, beginning in the 6th century BCE, before finally being written down around 500 CE.

DEISM
Definition, history, belief and practices

Deism is defined in Webster's Encyclopedic Dictionary as "The Doctrine or creed of a Deist." Deist is defined in the same dictionary as "One who believes in the existence of God or Supreme Being but denies revealed religion basing his belief on the right of nature and reason."

The word "Deism" is derived from the Latin word for God: "Deus."

Deists do not follow the fundamental beliefs of most religions that God revealed himself to humanity through the writings of the Bible, the Qur'an or other religious texts. Deists disagree with Atheists who assert that there is no evidence of the existence of God.

Deists regard their faith as a natural religion, rather with one that is revealed by a God or which is artificially created by humans. They reason that since everything that exists has had a creator, then God must have created the universe itself.

HISTORY OF DEISM

The term "Deism" originally referred to a belief in one deity, as compared with the belief in no God (Atheism) and belief in many Gods (Polytheism). During the later 17th century, "Deism" began to refer to forms of radical Christianity belief systems that rejected miracles, revelation, and the inerrancy of the Bible. Currently Deism is no longer associated with Christianity or any other e-established religion. Then, as now, Deism is not a religious movement in the conventional sense of the world.

There is no Deistic network of places of worship, a priesthood or hierarchy of authority.

Deism was greatly influential among politicians, scientists and philosophers during the late 17th and 18th century, in England, France, Germany and the United States.

Early Deism was a logical outgrowth of the great advances in astronomy, physics and chemistry that had been made by Bacon, Copernicus, Galileo and others. It was a small leap from rational study of nature to the application of the same techniques in religion. Early Deists believed that the Bible contained important truths, but they rejected the concept that it was divinely inspired or inerrant. They were leaders in the study of the Bible as a historical document rather than an inspired, revealed one. Lord Herbert of Cherbury (d.1648) was one of the earliest proponents of Deism in England. In his book "De Veritate" (1624), he described the "Five Articles" of English Deists: 1.) belief in the existence of a single supreme God, 2.) humanity's duty to revere God, 3.) linkage of worship with practical morality, 4.) God will forgive us if we repent and abandon our sins, 5.) good works will be rewarded (and punishment for evil) both in life and after death.

Other English Deists were Anthony Collins (1676-1729), Matthew Tindal (1657-1733). French Deists leaders were J.J. Rousseau (1712-1778) and Voltaire (1694-1778).

Many of the leaders of the French and American revolutions followed this belief system, including John Quincy Adams, Ethan Allen, Benjamin Franklin, Thomas Jefferson, James Madison, Thomas Paine and George Washington. Deists played a major role in creating the principle of separation of church and state, and the religious freedom clauses of the 1st Amendment of the Constitution.

BELIEFS AND PRACTICES

Most Deists believe that God created the universe, set it in motion and then disassociated himself from his creation. A few Deists believe that God still intervenes in human affairs from time to time. Deists believe God has not selected a chosen people (e.g. Jews or Christians) to be the recipients of any special revelation or gifts.

Deists deny the existence of the Trinity as conceived by Christians. They may view Jesus as a philosopher, teacher and healer, but not as the Son of God. Deists believe that miracles do not happen. Deists believe a practical morality can be derived from reason without the need to appeal to religious revelation and church dogma. Deists pray, but only to express their appreciation to God for his works.

OUR FOUNDING FATHERS WERE DEISTS

Many of our founding fathers, presidents and patriots were generally Deists or Unitarians, believing some form of impersonal divine guidance but rejecting the divinity of Jesus and many of the stories in the Old and New testaments.

THOMAS PAINE

Thomas Paine was a pamphleteer whose powerful writings (most notably Common Sense) helped the faltering spirits of the country and aided materially in winning the war of Independence. Paine was also a supporter of Deism, in which he voiced in his treatise on religion, *The Age of Reason*, in 1794 and various essays. In *The Age of Reason*, Paine stated: "*I do not believe in the creed professed by the Jewish church, by the Roman church, by the Greek church, by the Turkish church, by the Protestant church, nor by any church that I know of. My mind is my mind is my own church. All national institutions of churches, whether Jewish, Christian or Turkish, appear to me no other than human inventions, set up to terrify and enslave mankind, and monopolize power and profit.*" '*Each of those churches accuse the other of unbelief; and for my own, I disbelieve them all.*"

Another essay was published in 1804 by Paine entitled "*Of The Religion of Deism Compared With The Christian Religion*". A short excerpt of his essay is as follows: "*Every person, of whatever religious denomination he may be, is a DEIST in the first article of his Creed. Deism, from the Latin word Deus, God, is the belief of a God, and this belief is the first article of every man's creed.*

It is on this article, universally consented to by all mankind, that the Deist builds his church, and here he rests, Whenever we step aside from this article, by mixing it with articles of human invention, we wander in to a labyrinth of uncertainty and fable, and become exposed to every kind of imposition by pretenders to revelation.

. . . The Jew shows what he calls the law of Moses, given, he says, by God, on the Mount Sinai; the Christian shows a collection of

books and epistles, written by nobody knows who, and called the New Testament; and the Mahometan shows the Koran, given, he says, by God to Mahomet: each of these calls itself revealed religion, and the only true Word of God, and this the followers of each profess to believe from the habit of education, and each believes the others are imposed upon.

But when the divine gift begins to expand itself and calls man to reflection, he then reads and contemplates God and His works, and not in the books pretending to be revelation. The creation is the Bible of the true believer in God. Everything in this vast volume inspires him with sublime ideas of the Creator. The little and paltry, and often obscene, tales of the Bible sink into wretchedness when put in comparison with this mighty work.

The Deist needs none of those tricks and shows called miracles to confirm his faith, for what can be a greater miracle than the creation itself, and his own existence?

There is happiness in Deism, when rightly understood, that is not to be found in any other system of religion. All other systems have something in them that shock our reason, or are repugnant to it, and man, if he thinks at all, must stifle his reason in order to force himself to believe them.

But in Deism our reason and our belief become happily united. The wonderful structure of the universe, and everything we behold in the system of the creation, prove to us, far better than books can do, the existence of a God, and at the same time proclaim His attributes.

. . . Here it is that the religion of Deism is superior to the Christian Religion. It is free from all those invented and torturing articles that shock our reason or injure our humanity, and with which the Christian religion abounds, its creed is pure, and sublimely simple. It believes in God, and there it rests."

GEORGE WASHINGTON

George Washington, the first president of the United States, never declared himself a Christian according to contemporary reports or in any of his voluminous correspondence. According to Bishop William White, "truth requires me say that Gen. Washington never received communion in the churches of which I am parochial minister. The Reverend James Abercrombie, the other pastor of the congregation Washington attended, told The Reverend Bird Wilson, an Episcopal minister in Albany, New York, in 1831, that in regard to Washington's religious views, Abercrombie replied, "Sir, Washington was a Deist".

Washington championed the cause of freedom from religious intolerance and compulsion. When John Murray (a universalist who denied the existence of hell) was invited to become an army chaplain, the other chaplains petitioned Washington for his dismissal. Instead, Washington gave him the appointment. On his deathbed, Washington uttered no words of a religious nature and did not call for a clergyman to be in attendance.

In the book *Washington and Religion* by Paul F.Boller, Jr., Boiler includes a quote from a Presbyterian minister, Arthur B. Bradford, who was an associate of Ashbel Green another Presbyterian minister who had known George Washington personally. Bradford wrote that Green, "often said in my hearing, though very sorrowfully, of course, that while Washington was very deferential to religion and its ceremonies, like nearly all the founders of the Republic, he was not a Christian, but a Deist."

In February 1800, after Washington's death, Thomas Jefferson wrote this statement in his personal journal, "I know that Gouverneur Morris (principal drafter of the constitution), who claimed to be in his secrets, and believed him self to be so, has often told me that General Washington believed no more in that system (Christianity) than he did."

JOHN ADAMS

John Adams, the country's second president, was drawn to the study of law but faced pressure from his father to become a clergyman. He wrote that he found among lawyers "noble and gallant achievements" but among the clergy, the "pretended sanctity of some absolute dunces".

From a letter to Thomas Jefferson: "I almost shudder at the thought of alluding to the most fatal example of the abuses of grief which the history of mankind has preserved — the Cross. Consider what calamities that engine of grief has produced!"

From a letter to Charles Cushing (October 19, 1756): "Twenty times in the course of my late reading, have I been upon the point of breaking out, 'this would be the best of all possible worlds, if there were no religion in it."

It was during Adam's administration that the Senate ratified the Treaty of Peace and Friendship (Treaty of Tripoli, June 7, 1797). Article 11 states: "The government of the United States is not in any sense founded on the Christian religion."

From an excerpt of another letter, John Adams quotes, "The doctrine of the divinity of Jesus is made a convenient cover for absurdity."

Lastly, another quote, "The question before the human race is, whether the God of nature shall govern the world by his own laws, or whether priests and kings shall rule it by fictitious miracles."

THOMAS JEFFERSON

Thomas Jefferson, third president and author of the Declaration of Independence, said," I trust there is not a young man now living in the United States who will not die a Unitarian." He referred to the Revelation of St. John as "the ravings of a maniac" and wrote: "The Christian priesthood, finding the doctrines of Christ levelled to every understanding and too plain to need explanation, saw, in the mysticisms of Plato, materials with which they might build up an artificial system which might, from its indistinctness, admit everlasting controversy, give employment for their order, and introduce it to profit, power, and pre-eminence. The doctrines which flowed from the lips of Jesus himself are within the comprehension of a child; but thousands of volumes have not yet explained the Platonisms engrafted on them: and for this obvious reason that nonsense can never be explained." (letter to John Adams, July 5, 1814).

In a letter to William Short (from Notes on the State of Virginia, 1781-1782), Jefferson wrote, "I have examined all the known superstitions of the world, and I do not find in our particular superstition of Christianity one redeeming feature. They are all alike founded on fables and mythology. Millions of innocent men, women and children, since the introduction of Christianity, have been burnt, tortured, fined and imprisoned. What has been the effect of this coercion? To make one half the world fools and the other half hypocrites; to support roguery and error all over the earth."

Jefferson believed that God was the creator of the universe, of man, of morality; but the idea that God was an active presence in the world he dismissed as mere superstition. As for Jesus, although he was the greatest moral teacher, he was not divine, nor was the anointed servant of the divine.

Jefferson says he was a "Materialist" (letter to William Short, April 13, 1820) and a "Unitarian" (letter to Waterhouse, Jan. 8, 1825). Jefferson rejected the Christian doctrine of the "Trinity" (letter to Dërieux, July 25, 1788) as well as the doctrine of an eternal Hell (letter to Van der Kemp, May 1, 1817). Jefferson never stated "I am a Deist" in any of his writings but, Jefferson specifically named Joseph Priestly (English Unitarian who moved to America) and Conyers Middleton (English Deist) and said: "I rest on them... as the basis of my own faith" (letter to John Adams, August 22, 1813). Therefore, without using the actual words, Jefferson issued an authentic statement claiming Deism as his faith.

Jefferson was just as suspicious of the traditional belief that the Bible is "the inspired word of God." He rewrote the story of Jesus as told in the New Testament and compiled his own gospel version known as The Jefferson Bible, which eliminated all miracles attributed to Jesus and ended with his burial. In a letter to John Adams, he wrote, "To talk of immaterial existence is to talk of nothings. To say that the human soul, angels, God, is immaterial is to say they are nothings, or that there is no God, no angels, and no soul. I cannot reason otherwise" (August 15, 1820). In saying this, Jefferson was merely expressing the widely held Deistic view of his time, which rejected the mysticism of the Bible and relied on natural law and human reason to explain why the world is as it is. In another letter to Adams again, Jefferson said, "And the day will come when the mystical generation of Jesus, by the supreme being as his father in the womb of a virgin, will be classed with the fable of the generation of Minerva in the brain of Jupiter" (April 11, 1823).

In yet another letter, Jefferson states, "Christianity... (has become) the most perverted system that ever shone on man... Rogueries, absurdities and untruths were perpetrated upon the teachings of Jesus by a large band of dupes and importers led by Paul, the first great corrupter of the teaching of Jesus."

JAMES MADISON

James Madison, fourth president and father of the Constitution, was not religious in any conventional sense. In a letter William Bradford, April 1, 1774, "Religious bondage shackles and debilitates the mind and unfits it for every noble enterprise."

In his work Memorial and Remonstrance Against Religious Assessments, Section 7, 1785, "During almost fifteen centuries has the legal establishment of Christianity been on trial. What have been its fruits? More or less, in all places, pride and indolence in the clergy, ignorance and servility in laity; in both, superstition, bigotry, and persecution."

ETHAN ALLEN

Ethan Allen, is best known for the capture of Fort Ticonderoga while commanding the Green Mountain Boys helped inspire Congress and the country to pursue the War of Independence, said, "That Jesus Christ was not God is evidence from his own words." In the same book, Allen noted that he was generally "denominated a Deist, the reality of which I never disputed, being conscious that I am no Christian." When Ethan Allen married Fanny Buchanan, he stopped his own wedding ceremony when the judge asked him if he promised, "to live with Fanny Buchanan agreeable to the laws of God." Allen refused to answer until the judge agreed that the God referred to was the God of Nature, and the laws were those "written in the great book of nature."

BENJAMIN FRANKLIN

Delegate to the Continental Congress and the Constitutional Convention Benjamin Franklin said in his autobiography: "Scarcely was I arrived at fifteen years of age, when, after having doubted in turn of different tenets, according as I found them combated in the different books that I read. I began to doubt of Revelation itself"... "Some books against Deism fell into my hands... It happened that they wrought an effect on me quite contrary to what was intended by them; for the arguments of the Deists, which were quote to be refuted, appeared to me much stronger than the refutations, in short, I soon became a thorough Deist."

In a letter to Ezra Stiles, president of Yale (March 1, 1790), who had asked him his views on religion, Franklin replied, "As to Jesus of Nazareth, my Opinion of whom you particularly desire, I think the System of Morals and his Religion, as he left them to us, the best the world ever saw or is likely to see, but I apprehend it has received various corrupt changes, and I have, with most of the present Dissenters in England, some Doubts as to his divinity; tho' it is a question I do not dogmatize upon, having never studied it, and I think it needless to busy myself with it now, when I expect soon an Opportunity of knowing the Truth with less Trouble..." Franklin died just over a month later on April 17th.

OTHER FAMOUS DEISTS – ABRAHAM LINCOLN

Abraham Lincoln was a Deist in his youth, but was subsequently, and probably wisely, advised against advertising that fact if he wanted to succeed in politics. Legend has him converting to Christianity, though Lincoln himself never bothered to mention it to anyone. No one else mentioned it either until long after Lincoln's death. And no one agrees on where or when his supposed profound life changing took place. Depending on the source, it was either in Illinois or Washington, in 1848, 1858, 1862, or 1863. Such large discrepancies make "never" the most likely. Lincoln's closest friend and law partner for over twenty years, William H. Herndon, claimed that Lincoln had no religious beliefs at all. Lincoln's own silence on the subject makes his friend's observation seem probable.

Furthermore, Colonel Ward H. Lamon published his book, *Life of Abraham Lincoln* in 1872. Colonel Lamon had the advantage of being Lincoln's friend and acquaintance of years. When Lincoln passed away Lamon had the benefit of the collection of manuscripts pertaining to Lincoln gathered by William H. Herndon, who knew the real Lincoln better than any other man. Lamon states, "Mr. Lincoln was never a member of any Church, nor did he believe in the divinity of Christ, or the inspiration of the Scriptures in the sense understood by evangelical Christians."

Lamon had other witnesses to reinforce his own statements about Lincoln's religious beliefs. The last witness quoted by Colonel Lamon is Mrs. Mary Todd Lincoln, wife of Abraham Lincoln. She states, "Mr. Lincoln had no hope, and no faith, in the usual acceptation of those words." She also added, "Mr. Lincoln's maxim and philosophy were: 'What is to be, will be, and no prayers of ours can arrest the decree.' He never joined any Church. He was a religious man always, I think, but was not a technical Christian."

OTHER FAMOUS DEISTS – CARL SAGAN

Dr. Carl Edward Sagan, was a noted American astronomer, astrobiologist and highly successful science popularizer. He pioneered exobiology and promoted the Search for Extra-Terrestrial Intelligence (SETI). He is world-famous for his popular science books and award-winning television series Cosmos, which he co-wrote and presented and eventually released as a book.

After giving a speech in New York in 1993 during the Earth Mass festivities, a Christian reporter who had previously considered him an atheist, asked Sagan if his religious views have evolved in recent years, to which Sagan replied, "I remain inexorably opposed to any kind of revealed religion and reject any talk of a personal god, but millions of people believe in a god that is not that kind of god. Some might say, for example, that there is some kind of force or power in the watch — a set of laws, perhaps. Then the watch creates itself. I'm more comfortable with that kind of language."

Carl Sagan once stated, "A religion that stressed the magnificence of the universe as revealed by modern science, might be able to draw forth reserves of reverence and awe hardly tapped by traditional faiths. Sooner or later, such a religion will emerge."

FREEMASONS – History, Beliefs and Practices

The first Grand Lodge of England was founded in 1717, marking the founding of the modern era of Freemasonry.

The first American Lodges were chartered by British Lodges, but as time went on American Lodges also began chartering new Lodges.

The Bible is the "Volume of Sacred Law" of most Western Lodges. It is one of the three objects comprising "The Three Great Lights," the most common and important Masonic symbol, which must be displayed while Lodges meet. The other objects are the compass and the square, and the sacred volume, which does not have to be the Bible. It may be whatever scripture is revered by the members of the Lodge.

Freemasonry is not a religion. It is a fraternal order, although many Christian ideas and ideals are important to the Masons and are incorporated in their rituals. To become a Mason one must ask a friend in the Lodge to recommend him, and all the members must vote unanimously on the acceptance. The requirement for membership is a belief in one non-specific Supreme Being.

Freemasonry's basic tenets are: 1.) brotherly love (tolerance, respect, kindness and understanding of others, especially to their Masonic Brothers). 2.) relief (caring for the whole community through philanthropy; example is their charitable work of Shriner's hospitals) and 3.) truth (morals).

These basic tenets, when followed, should achieve a higher standard of life for the Masons. Masons build character by contact with the company and shared morals of their "Brothers" (fellow members). It has religious undertones because of this stress on morality. Since Freemasonry is a fraternity, it also stresses the fellowship and enjoyable company of its brothers in social activities such as dinners, picnics and lectures on Masonic history.

There are three levels that joining Masons must advance through by memorizing a small amount of material that varies from jurisdiction to jurisdiction. The levels are called degrees. The first degree is Entered Apprentice, the second, Fellow Craft, and the third is Master Mason. The head of the Lodge is called the Worshipful Master. Becoming a mason usually takes a few months in the United States, but a mandatory three years in England.

Masons are restricted from talking about religion or politics in the Lodges because these are controversial topics known to divide men. Having a religion is encouraged, although there is no specific one recommended. Christianity, however, seems to prevail in the United States.

FOUNDING FATHERS THAT WERE FREEMASONS

Many of our founding fathers attended Freemasonry lodges. According to John J. Robinson, "Freemasonry had been a powerful force for religious freedom." Freemasons took seriously the principle that men should worship according to their own conscious. Masonry welcomed anyone from any religion or non-religion, as long as they believed in a Supreme Being. George Washington, Benjamin Franklin, John Hancock, Alexander Hamilton and many others accepted Freemasonry.

PART III
INTELLIGENT LIFE ON OTHER PLANETS AND RELIGION

It is estimated that there are over 100 billion galaxies in the universe and that each galaxy contains around 100 billion stars. So the number of stars in the universe is roughly 100 billion x 100 billion or 10 sextillion (that's 1 with 22 zeros after it, or 10 thousand billion billion). There have been over 300 stars with confirmed extrasolar planets (exoplanets) discovered to date. Researchers who work on exoplanets theorize that planets which are similar to Earth may be discovered at some point.

If and when intelligent life is discovered in the universe what implications will this discovery have on religion? There are many questions one could ask — are they fallen like us? Did they have their own version of Adam and Eve? Did they have a savior? What if intelligent life discovered a planet that believes in no God, does that mean there is a Godless universe. Do aliens have a soul? What if the aliens have their own religion and wanted to convert us to their God? What if they have their own prophet?

There are even some theories one called 'the Jesus Seed" a wild theory, which speculates that perhaps, every planet that harbors intelligent, self-aware life may also have had a Christ walk on their planet, just as Jesus supposedly did here on Earth.

Other questions one would ask especially of the Christian faith — Is original sin something that affects all intelligent beings? Is Jesus Christ's redemptive sacrifice sufficient for the whole universe? Would there be a parallel history of salvation on other planets?

With the different scenarios possible one can at least state that God would remain the creator of the universe but the way we think about revealed religion (The Bible, Qur'an, The Torah) and various prophets could change.

If we discovered an intelligent life on another planet and that planet's alien life had a structured religion in that they believe in God but had no Bible, Koran, etc, and did not believe in Jesus Christ or Mohammed or any of the prophets on Earth, and even believed in good over evil, do we dare say with our arrogance that our religious beliefs on the planet Earth is superior and correct and that their religious beliefs are wrong or do we advance to the next level and admit perhaps some of our details of our religious beliefs might be too narrow minded, maybe satisfactory for the planet Earth but realize that their religious views is just as important to them as ours to us. In other words mankind will experience a religious revolution, just like back 350 years ago when we thought the Sun moved around the Earth and Galileo showed us that was wrong, that the Earth orbited the Sun.

As science advances one can come closer to God. Revealed religion can change and they can come and go. Look at the Mormon religion; they added a version of the Bible with a new prophet just over 150 years ago. But one thing remains constant in religion in that there is a belief in a Supreme Being and he is creator of the universe.

One can have faith in God, but still believe in science and technology. On can believe that God flicked a switch, triggering an almighty explosion some 10 billion plus years ago (Big Bang Theory) and allowing his creation to unfold in accordance with his omniscient plan. Science explains how God did it; science is not trying to take away Religion, but rather give us a better insight into Religion.

The discovery of extraterrestrial life will not destroy religion but will evolve religion. It will help discard the bad ideas in religion, the narrow views, the medieval beliefs (that it's this way or no way). Perhaps we will realize that God accepts different religious views. We might realize that our revealed religions on Earth need reworking as we discover other intelligent life and learn of their religious beliefs (if any).

Perhaps instead of spending time trying to convince others that this particular religious view is the only correct view for ones' salvation, maybe they rather learn to accept and embrace different viewpoints and realize that even though different revealed religions have different beliefs, histories and prophets, that one must remember that the underlying universal constant is simply, God, creator of the universe, good over evil, and love thy neighbor can be found by all.

PART FOUR: COMMON FACTORS OF RELIGION, EVOLUTION OF RELIGION, SCIENCE AND RELIGION, EVOLUTION OF NEW RELIGIONS

Let's examine the common factors of religion: Most all religions have prophets or teachers. Islam has a prophet named Muhammad, Christianity has a prophet named Jesus (the Mormons, a branch of Christianity has the prophet Joseph Smith), Baha'i believe God sent nine prophets (Abraham, Krishna, Moses, Zoroaster, Buddha, Jesus Christ, Muhammad, The Bab and Baha Ullah), Judaism greatest prophets are Abraham and Moses (Judaism believes The Torah was revealed to Moses by God), Buddhism has the teachings of Siddhartha Gautama (Buddha), Zoroastnanism has the prophet Zoroaster (Zarathustra), Confucianism has the teachings of K'ung Fu Tzu (Confucius), Janism has the teachings of 24 Tirthankaras (Prophets of Janism) who have gained omniscence, Taoism has the teachings of Lao-Tse (a contemporary of Confucius in China), Sikhism has the teachings of Sri Guru Nanak Dev Ji (Guru Nanak), Shinto has no prophet or teacher but has various "Kami" nature deities and though Hinduism doesn't have any specific prophets they do believe that whenever profound evil spreads widely throughout the earth, the Supreme Being comes to earth in the form of a human person; Lord Kriskna was just such an incarnation. Krishna was the eighth incarnation of Vishnu (the Godhead of Hindu Trinity of deities).

All the religions have one particular Holy Book or sacred texts. The texts of the Holy Books is believed to have been revealed by God, Christianity has the Bible (New Testament and the Old Testament), the Mormons (branch of Christianity) has The Book of Mormon: Another Testament of Jesus Christ, Judaism has the Tanakh (often referred to as the Old Testament by Christians) which is composed of The Torah (Five Books of Moses) and two other group of books, Buddhism generally accepts the Tripitaka (Pali Canon), Hinduism's most sacred scriptures are the Vedas ("Book of Knowledge"), Sikhism has the Guru Granth Sahib (also known as the Adi Granth), Baha'i faith has the Kitab-i-Aqba (The Most Holy Book), Taoism has the Tao-te Ching (Classic of the Way of Power), Confucianism has the Lun-Yu (Analects), Shinto has the Kojiki (Records of Ancient Matters) and the Nihongi (Chronicles of Japan) which are in a sense the sacred books, Jainism's sacred texts are called Agamas and Islam has the Qur'an. Prayer and worship is basic to all religions although the methods may be different.

All religions believe in the principle of a soul or the spirit, the afterlife. Hinduism believes in addition of having a soul, that one can return in human form again (reincarnation).

All religions believe in God and Evil and a Heaven and Hell. Zoroastrians however believe Hell is temporary where sinners are cleansed by fire (similar to the Catholic concept of purgatory).

All religions believe in the equality of man. All are children of God. All are equal.

All religions have rules and stress the necessity of ethical life. Morality is an important pre-requisite for a religious life.

All religions emphasize on the necessity and value of sacrifice; on helping your neighbor.

All religions emphasize the brotherhood of man that man should love his fellow being and all the creation. All religions believe in being good, and doing good.

All religions have an ultimate goal of making man perfect. Man is incomplete without religion. Religion unites man with God.

All religions believe in a Supreme Being and that God created the universe.

EVOLUTION OF RELIGION

The major religions have evolved over time facing conflicts of their particular religious dogma, sometimes causing religious splits or religious wars. Several examples of evolution of religion are described below beginning with Christianity. Christianity faced a major conflict in 325 CE at the Council of Nicea, concerning the relationship between Jesus and God. There were conflicting theories about the deity of Jesus. One group led by Anus believed that Jesus and God were separate and different. They believed Jesus was created by God and therefore at one point did not exist and that he was not divine. The other group led by Athansasius believed that Jesus was one with God, the same substance as God the Father and eternal.

It was ultimately decided that Jesus Christ was "of one substance with the Father". Over the next few centuries more Council meetings were held to resolve major conflicts of the Christian church.

The Roman Catholic Church and the Eastern Orthodox Church became increasingly remote from each other until a formal split occurred in 1054 CE. Each contended that it more correctly maintains the tradition of the early church and that the other had deviated.

In 1517, Martin Luther, a Christian Monk from Germany, said that the Roman Catholic Church was corrupt and that it should be reformed so that it was less greedy, fairer and accessible to all people, not just the rich and well educated. A split followed, producing the Protestant Reformation. Unfortunately a series of religious wars began which decimated Western Europe. Protestantism eventually split into many movements which themselves split into families of denominations. Currently there are thousands of individual Protestant denominations and sects that we observe today.

Hinduism gradually divided into three great classes, the Vaishnavas, the Saivas and the Saktas. Hinduism also underwent a reform in the 18th and 19th century making progressive changes. Some of these reforms included contributing to more education for women, making ritualism optional, ending child marriages and rejecting worship of idols of numerous gods, supporting equal rights for of man and woman, and supported inter-caste marriage. The caste system originally mentioned in the Rig Vegas affixed five social castes. One's caste determined the range of jobs or professions from which one could choose. People were born into the same caste of their parents. There was no mobility across caste lines during one's lifetime. The five castes were Brahmins (Priests and Religious officials), Kshatriyas (Rulers and Military), Vaishyas (Farmers and Merchants), Sudras (Peasants and Servants) and Harijan (the Untouchables). Over time the Caste system had led to segregation and untouchability. The caste system was abolished in 1949 by the Indian government.

The original unity of Buddhism began to fragment a few centuries after Buddha's death. Several schools and traditions arose. Most of them ceased to exist being absorbed by others and today we have three main schools of Buddhism each having different traditions. Theravada (Southern Buddhism) is the oldest school, formed around 250 BCE. Mahayana (Northern Buddhism) was formed around 100 CE. Vajrayana (Tibetan, Eastern Buddhism) was formed in the 7th century CE.

The Islam religion underwent a Sunni-Shiite split around 632 when the prophet Muhammad died. There was a dispute over who was to lead the Muslim community and how the leader was to be chosen. According to Shiite tradition, the Prophet Muhammad made claims, also in a famous speech delivered at his last pilgrimage, that All was to succeed him as leader of the Muslim community. The Sunni account of this speech includes everything but the proclamation of all as successor. After the Prophets' death, a gathering of Muslims at Saqifah gave their allegiance to Abu Bakrr, as the first calip due to his close relationship with the Prophet. Shiite Muslims believe that the Prophet had appointed his son-in-law All ibn Abi Talib as his successor and that in following Abu Bakr, the Sunni Muslims had strayed from the true path.

Thirty years after Muhammad's death the Islamic community plunged into the First Islamic civil war. This civil war led to the emergence of two distinct Islamic groups: Sunnis and the Shiite.

The Baha'i religion was founded in 1844 by Mirza Ali Muhamed who took on the title of the "Bab". The "Bab's" teachings spread throughout Iran, causing much resistance from the Shiite Muslim Clergy and the government. Consequently, the "Bab" was arrested, incarcerated and executed in 1850. In addition, 20,000 Babi followers were also executed. Currently there are over five million followers of the Baha'i faith in the world with between 150,000 to 300,000 still in Iran. Members of the Baha'l faith in Iran are still discriminated and encounter violence against them.

Principal form of Judaism that developed after the fall of the Second Temple of Jerusalem (70 CE) was Rabbinic Judaism. It originated in the teaching of the Pharisees, who emphasized the need for the critical interpretation of the Torah. Rabbinic Judaism (today, know simply as "Judaism") developed into several distinct denominations in late 18th century Europe: Reform Judaism, Liberal Judaism, many forms of Orthodox Judaism and Conservative Judaism.

The newest Jewish movement to emerge is Reconstructionist Judaism which was developed in the late I920s to the 1940s.

Jainism began as a Hindu reform movement, but became an independent religion by the 6th century. Jains divided into two major sects: the Digambara and the Svetambara. They disagree on details of the life of Mahavflra, the spiritual status of women, whether monks should wear clothes (Digambara monks live completely naked), rituals and which texts should be accepted as scripture.

Sikh faith evolved into several sects who are not recognized by the majority of Sikhs as orthodox in their teachings and beliefs.

Shinto evolved in four main forms or traditions: Kooshitsu Shinto, Shrine Shinto (largest Shinto group, it was the original form of the religion; dating back to the beginning of Japanese history), Folk Shinto and Sect Shino.

Shinto is the newest form of Shinto, founded by individuals at the start of the 19th century. Sect Shinto consists of 12 sects; each has its own beliefs and doctrines.

Religious Taoism originated in China and as the religion grew the succession of teachers of Chiang Ling (the founder of Religious Taoism) began practicing more diverse and elaborate ceremonies and rituals. Religious Taoism failed to establish a central authority and as a result, religious Taoism broke into many sects. While the sects refer back to Lao Tse (founder of Taoism), they all placed a different emphasis on the scriptures and had their own unique ritualistic ceremonies. As a result of the number of sects, religious Taoism experienced a large loss of followers.

Confucianism diverged after the death of its founder Confucius. The followers of Confucius began developing the Confucian doctrine in different directions. Different schools of Confucianism developed in different timelines: Scholastic Confucianism in the Han dynasty (206 BCE-220 BCE), Neo-Confucianism in the Song Dynasty (960-1279 CE).

Schools of Confucianism developed in Korea (Korean Confucianism), Japan (Japanese Confucianism) and Singapore (Singapore Confucianism). New Confucianism is a new movement of Confucianism that began in the 20th century. It is deeply influenced by Neo-Confucianism of the Song and Ming dynasties.

All the major religions evolved over time by splitting into groups, denominations, schools or sects. Religion has had to adapt and make changes in order to survive in our society.

SCIENCE AND RELIGION

Fear had been used in the past to keep believers attached to religious doctrines, to maintain the Status Quo and to inhibit ambitious thinkers. People who persisted with wrong thoughts ran the risk of being excommunicated or even killed.

Galileo Galilei was a famous 17th century Italian scientist who made himself one of the world's first telescopes and discovered the moons of Jupiter. During Galileo's time most people believed that the earth was the center of the universe and that the sun revolved around the earth. However, Galileo supported Copernicus' theory that the earth revolved around the sun. This brought him in conflict with the Catholic Church. By threatening him with torture, the Church forced him to recant his views in front of a tribunal and sentenced him to house arrest. However, Galileo's trials and theories inspired others like Newton and Kepler to prove that the earth was not the center of the universe.

In 1992 Pope John Paul II publicly admitted that the church had made a mistake in condemning Galileo. Creation science was the prevailing belief system for Christians before the rise of geology in the late 18th Century. The early European scientists, from Copernicus to Galileo to Newton believed in a literal interpretation of the Bible's account of creation. Bishop Usher's date of October 22, 4004 BCE was generally accepted among Christian scientists until early 18th century, when it became obvious to most researchers that geological processes were exceedingly slow, and must have been accomplished over incredibly long periods of time. A 6000-year-old earth was just not possible.

As geologists promoted theories about the earth's age, opposition arose in many religious organizations. Friction increased between science and technology when Darwin published *The Origin of Species By Means of Natural Selection* in 1859 *and The Descent of Man* in 1871. Many mainstream and liberal clergy found evolutionary theory compatible with their faith, however the conservative clerics considered it blasphemous.

The Catholic Church in the early 1950's began to teach that the Genesis creation story should not interpreted literally, but symbolically.

The official Catholic stance is that evolution is not incompatible with faith. The Vatican is organizing a conference to mark the 200th anniversary of the birth of the author of the *Origin of Species*, Charles Darwin.

Creationism is still the belief held by Fundamental and Evangelical Christians, all the denominations of conservative Protestantism, traditional Catholicism, Orthodox Judaism, conservative Islam and other monotheistic religions.

Evolutionism is the basic premise of many religions, including Buddhism, Confucianism, Hinduism, Taoism, Liberal Protestantism, Modernist Catholicism, Reform Judaism and others.

Believing in evolution does not take away the existence of God. One can still believe in God and take a view of either God played a role in evolution or let evolution be driven by blind, purely natural forces.

EVOLUTION OF NEW RELIGIONS

The United States saw new developments in religion in the 19th century. Sects (small religious group that has branched off of a larger established religion) and movements of many types sprang up, inspired by new interpretations of the Bible, the teachings of new prophets and thinkers, the expectations of Jesus Christ's second coming, and the social, scientific and philosophical questions of the time.

Christian Science was founded by Mary Baker Eddy in 1879. Christian Science views creation as entirely spiritual. The church holds the Bible as authorative yet interprets it in a distinct way, focusing on the life of Jesus as a model of healing by prayer, a necessary element of spiritual growth. According to Christian Science, physical illness and injury result from error or wrong belief and be healed through one's own prayer or through the ministration of a Christian Science practitioner.

Joseph Smith Jr. established the Church of Jesus Christ of Latter-day Saints in 1830. He described an encounter with an angel who gave him the text that would become the Book of Mormon. The Mormon's believe that the second coming of Jesus Christ will lead to a chain of events that will result in a final resurrection, after which earth will become a celestial home for all people.

Charles Taze Russell founded Jehovah's Witnesses in 1872. After studying the Bible for a period of time, he concluded that the invisible return of Christ had occurred in 1874 and that Jesus Christ would rule as king in 1914 (a date they believe was prophesized in Scripture), that Jehovah's witnesses were selected by God to be his people and following a war, the kingdom of God would be established on earth. Jehovah's Witnesses no longer set such specific dates but believe God's kingdom of a government of divine guidance will follow Armageddon, the great war described in prophetic books of the Bible. They believe that biblical prophecies are being fulfilled in world events and that Jesus was created by God and acts as his agent.

A recent sect, Scientology was created by L. Ron Hubbard (an American pulp fiction and science fiction writer) in 1952 as a self-help philosophy that took ideas from his earlier self-help system, Dianetics. Hubbard later described itself as a new religion.

Scientology claims to offer "an exact methodology" to help humans achieve awareness of their Spiritual existence across many lifetimes and to become effective in the physical world.

A number of governments now view the Church of Scientology as a religious organization, but others view it as simply a cult.

The beginning ideas to start these sects or religions needed only to reach prominence in the minds of their creators. As other followers took up these new sects or religions, new ideas were added, old ideas were changed or discarded, and thus the sect or religion evolves.

SUMMARY

Finding intelligent life exists in the universe would mean that we are not the center of the universe. For Christianity, Judaism and Islam the existence of aliens creates a problem.

All these religions are based on the idea of a covenant between us and God.

Now consider two possibilities: 1) the aliens do not believe in God and do not share the idea of a fall from grace by man and a promise between God and man of a way to return to grace and the forgiveness of sin. Perhaps they have a different religious belief of their own or 2) the aliens do believe in these things and even have a Moses, Jesus, or Mohammad of their own.

In addition some religious groups would believe these aliens would be in need of conversion and salvation, and of course it would be up to the faithful to lead the way. Some fundamental groups might lead to a new level of arrogance and self-righteousness believing they have a mission. Will our religion adopt a policy of non-interference concerning the alien's beliefs or will we try to convert them to our religious beliefs?

For the Christian faith the covenant was fulfilled in the sacrifice of Jesus Christ. Now if aliens had there own incarnation this would undermine the covenant we share with god and our personal savior. This would cause all kinds of problems for the doctrine of resurrection (do aliens and humans share the same kind of spirit). The existence of aliens would have the more fundamental effect on these monotheistic faiths of calling into question mans very relationship with God and the rest of creation.

Non-monotheistic religions would probably fair better, these would not be concerned with salvation or redemption, but with a universal spirit, or some such corresponding idea that the existence of aliens may be seen as just another manifestation of this universal life force.

NEW DEISM
AND THE FUTURE
OF RELIGION

Religion has undergone changes throughout our history and will continue to update itself as science and technology advances. Interpretation of religious scriptures will become less literal and more abstract in the future society, though core beliefs such as a Supreme Being, God created the universe, love thy neighbor, will remain the same.

The new age of Deism has been reborn for the 21st century and hence the term "New Deism" is used for the rebirth of Deism for the 21st century.

The argument of MY WAY OR NO WAY would NOT be true for a New Deist. A New Deist believes YOUR WAY EQUALS MY WAY in that no particular religion is any better than another religion and that one is allowed to take a different road to achieve one with God. In short, a New Deist respects all religions. It doesn't matter whether a New Deist agrees with a person's specific religious beliefs, only that a basic belief in a Supreme Being is a common factor.

A New Deist believes Church is not a requirement to be one with God. A New Deist believes Church (God) is in you, yourself. A New Deist does not believe that one has to accept Jesus Christ as your savior to go to Heaven, as is the requirement of many denominations of the Christian faith, but that one has only to believe in God and live a good life to achieve one with God.

A New Deist doesn't use any revealed religions (requiring a Holy Book or sacred texts) or a particular prophet as a basis for their belief. Instead a New Deist uses the rational mind in believing in a Supreme Being and that he is the creator of the universe.

A New Deist differs from a traditional Deist (Supreme Being created the universe, set it in operation and takes no further interest in it or humanity) in that a New Deist believes that God may take an active interest in the universe and humanity.

The future of religion is changing in the 21st century.

Father Funes, director of the Vatican Observatory near Rome says that intelligent beings created by God could exist in the universe. Funes also states that the existence of extraterrestrial life does not contradict belief in God. Fune believes that science and religion need each other.

As religion advances in the 21st century, the underlying constant in Religion though is simple: belief in God, the Supreme Being, creator of the universe and love thy neighbor.

Made in the USA
San Bernardino, CA
18 January 2019